Honeybee

Fox Squirrel

Cactus Wren

Ruby-throated Hummingbird

Gourami

American Alligator

Platypus

Elf Owl

African Gray Tree Frog

Ovenbird

Dusky Scrubfowl

Baya Weaver

Kemp's Ridley Sea Turtle

Bee Hummingbird

Black-tailed Prairie Dog

American Flamingo

Organ-pipe Mud Dauber

Lamprey

Bald-faced Hornet

Blue Jay

Orangutan

Buff-breasted Paradise Kingfisher

Cave Swiftlet

Army Ant

To Danny and Melissa, and to Samantha, Madison, and Jackson. —D. H. A.

To my parents, Frank and Marion Carlisle,
who successfully fledged five raucous nestlings. —S. L.

Library of Congress Cataloging-in-Publication Data:

Aston, Dianna Hutts, author.
A nest is noisy / by Dianna Aston ; illustrated by Sylvia Long.
pages cm
Audience: Ages 5–8.
Audience: K to grade 3.
ISBN 978-1-4521-2713-2 (alk. paper)
1. Nests—Juvenile literature. 2. Animals—Habitations—Juvenile literature.
3. Animal behavior—Juvenile literature. I. Long, Sylvia, illustrator. II. Title.

QL676.2.A835 2015
591.56'4—dc23
2013047998

Manufactured in China.

MIX
Paper from
responsible sources
FSC® C104723
FSC
www.fsc.org

Book design by Sara Gillingham Studio.
Hand lettered by Anne Robin and Sylvia Long.
The illustrations in this book were rendered in watercolor.

10 9 8 7 6 5 4 3 2 1

Chronicle Books LLC
680 Second Street
San Francisco, California 94107

Chronicle Books—we see things differently. Become part of our community at www.chroniclekids.com.

Orangutan

A Nest Is Noisy

Dianna Hutts Aston + Sylvia Long

chronicle books · san francisco

A nest is noisy.

It is a nursery of

chirp-chirping . . . .

Ruby-throated Hummingbird

Honeybee

buzzing . . .   *squeaking* . . .

American Alligator

Fox Squirrel

peep-peeping . . .

Gourami

bubbling . . .

babies.

A nest is welcoming.

Many birds assemble a cradle for their eggs, knitting together leaves and twigs, and softening it with grass, hair, moss, fluffy seeds, leaf skeletons, or even a snake's old skin. They might also add candy wrappers, plastic bags, and bits of cloth or paper.

Blue Jay

Birds are not the only animals that make nests. Orangutans climb high into the rainforest canopy, where each day they braid a new bed of strong branches and line it with a mattress of leaves and twigs. On rainy nights, a woven umbrella of leaves keeps them dry.

A nest is enormous . . .

One of the largest bird's nests
is the dusky scrubfowl's. Their
mounded nests are made of decomposing
leaves and twigs that can measure
more than 36 feet (11 metres) in diameter
and nearly 16 feet (5 metres) high.

Dusky Scrubfowl

1'   2'   3'   5'   6'   7'   8'   9'   10'   11'   12'   13'   14'   15'   16'   17'

or tiny.

Bee Hummingbird

The smallest bird's nest—the
bee hummingbird's—is a golf ball-size
cup of moss, lichen, bark, and leaves,
usually wrapped in spider's silk.
The stretchy silk lets the nest expand
as the babies grow larger.

1"   2"   3"   4"

20' 21' 22' 23' 24' 25' 26' 27' 28' 29' 30' 31' 32' 33' 34' 35'

A nest is spiky...

Elf owls and cactus wrens
select a prickly nesting place as
a refuge from slithering snakes
and other hungry hunters.

Elf Owl

Cactus Wren

Bald-faced Hornet

papery...

Hornets, yellow jackets, and paper wasps scrape fibers from weathered wood and chew it until it's a moist paste that dries into a tough, paper-like material. The bald-faced hornet queen makes a cell for each egg.

pebbly...

Eel-like lampreys use their suction-cup mouths to move stones the size of peas, walnuts, and even base-balls, and create depressions, called *redds*, in shallow streambeds. They lay their eggs in the redds, and cover them with more pebbles to hide them.

Lamprey

or even

African Gray Tree Frog

African gray tree frogs make a foamy nest
for their eggs in branches overhanging water. With
her hind legs, the female churns a substance
secreted from her body into a frothy mass that,
in sunlight, hardens into a meringue-like crust.
A few days after the tadpoles hatch, the nest
disintegrates and the tadpoles drop into the water
where they can feed and develop into frogs.

bubbly!

Gourami

Gourami blow bubbles that pack together to form a nest that floats like a raft in still water. Under the bubble nest, the male and female *spawn*—produce eggs. Once the female has released her eggs, she swims away while the male carries the eggs in his mouth and places them in the nest. After they hatch, the baby fish, or fry, swim beneath the gooey nests, where they are guarded by the male until they are ready to strike out on their own.

Ovenbird

Some South American ovenbirds forge an
adobe "oven" made with thousands of
mud and clay pellets. Baked in the sun,
the nest is a cozy place for their eggs.

A nest

An alligator piles decaying plants and mud to create a mat. In the center she digs a hole, where she lays her eggs and then, with her forelimbs and jaws, covers the nest with more vegetation to keep them warm until they hatch as squeaking babies. The temperature of the nest determines the sex of alligators.

is hot.

American Alligator

Kemp's Ridley Sea Turtle

A nest is hidden.

In spring and summer, tens of thousands of female Kemp's ridley sea turtles ride the waves together onto Gulf Coast beaches and drag themselves up to the dunes. They use their hind flippers like shovels to dig a pit in the sand. After the turtle deposits her round, leathery eggs, she tamps down the sand with the underside of her shell and flings more sand over the nest to hide any signs of it.

The platypus—one of only two mammals to lay eggs—hollows out tunnels or burrows along streambeds. With her tail, the female carries moist plant matter deep into the tunnel to make a nest and lays soft-shelled eggs the size of marbles. She adds plugs of soil in the tunnel to protect the eggs from rising waters, predators, and changing temperatures.

Platypus

A nest is neighborly.

There is safety in numbers. Some nest-builders
live in colonies, where there are more ears and
eyes to raise an alarm when *predators*—animals
that eat other animals—are near.

Baya Weaver

Baya weavers build nests that hang from thorny trees or palm fronds like upside-down bottles. Swinging in the air from a woven tube, each nest is protected from lizards, snakes, and bigger birds.

In "towns" of hundreds of inhabitants, black-tailed prairie dogs make grass-lined nesting chambers within the labyrinth of burrows. When a predator is spotted, the prairie dogs bark to warn their neighbors that danger is near.

Black-tailed Prairie Dog

Army ants make "living nests" called
bivouacs. Clinging to one another's legs and
jaws, or *mandibles*, they form a writhing
ball of millions of ants, suspended from
a branch by a chain of more ants. Inside
are chambers for the queen, a brood of
eggs, newly hatched larvae, and food.

A nest

Army Ant

Cave Swiftlet

is peculiar.

Cave swiftlets concoct a nest made
entirely of saliva. Swinging its head from side
to side, the male spits long, pearly strands
onto the wall of a cave that harden into a lacy
bowl when exposed to air. Bird's nest soup,
made from swiftlet nests, is among the most
expensive foods eaten by humans.

A nest

is muddy.

Flamingos erect a heap of mud, grass, and
stones up to 12 inches (30.5 centimetres) tall and then
lay a single egg in a depression at the top. The
height protects the egg from changing water levels
and excessive ground heat. Both parents feed their
hatchlings "crop milk" from their digestive tracts
until they leave the nest.

American Flamingo

A nest is adopted.

Some creatures choose nests made
by others to brood their offspring.
Cowbirds and common cuckoos lay their
eggs in nests of other birds, where
they are hatched and raised by the
mother of a different species.

The buff-breasted paradise kingfisher
flies like a torpedo at a termite
nest, smashing into the hard mound with
its beak (and sometimes dying on
impact!) to blast a hole into the side.
Inside the mound, they peck out a
tunnel leading to a chamber, where they
lay their eggs. Termites seal off the
tunnel from the inside, so that their
nests are separate.

Buff-breasted Paradise Kingfisher

Organ-pipe Mud Dauber

A nest is noisy...

Buzzing,
swishing,
rustling,
flapping,
and humming
with babies...

American Flamingo

Kemp's Ridley Sea Turtle

Black-tailed Prairie Dog

*but only until they are ready
to fly, swim, or crawl away.*

Then a nest is . . .

quiet.

Ruby-throated Hummingbird

Platypus

Blue Jay

Dusky Scrubfowl

Army Ant

Baya Weaver

Buff-breasted Paradise Kingfisher

Kemp's Ridley Sea Turtle

Gourami

Fox Squirrel

American Alligator

Bald-faced Hornet

Elf Owl

African Gray Tree Frog

Ovenbird

Cave Swiftlet

Black-tailed Prairie Dog

Honeybee

Bee Hummingbird

Orangutan

Cactus Wren

American Flamingo

Organ-pipe Mud Dauber

Lamprey